LAND OF NARRATIONS

HAIQA MOHD. IMRAN BHAT

Copyright © Haiqa Mohd. Imran Bhat
All Rights Reserved.

This book has been self-published with all reasonable efforts taken to make the material error-free by the author. No part of this book shall be used, reproduced in any manner whatsoever without written permission from the author, except in the case of brief quotations embodied in critical articles and reviews.

The Author of this book is solely responsible and liable for its content including but not limited to the views, representations, descriptions, statements, information, opinions and references ["Content"]. The Content of this book shall not constitute or be construed or deemed to reflect the opinion or expression of the Publisher or Editor. Neither the Publisher nor Editor endorse or approve the Content of this book or guarantee the reliability, accuracy or completeness of the Content published herein and do not make any representations or warranties of any kind, express or implied, including but not limited to the implied warranties of merchantability, fitness for a particular purpose. The Publisher and Editor shall not be liable whatsoever for any errors, omissions, whether such errors or omissions result from negligence, accident, or any other cause or claims for loss or damages of any kind, including without limitation, indirect or consequential loss or damage arising out of use, inability to use, or about the reliability, accuracy or sufficiency of the information contained in this book.

Made with ♥ on the Notion Press Platform
www.notionpress.com

I'm passionate about reading, writing, painting, and gymnastics. My journey into writing began when Khushnoor published her first book, which inspired me to explore my own creative side. Over time, I started entering writing competitions and was fortunate enough to be selected for several of them.

Contents

Contents

Preface

The book is filled with a variety of poems and stories, each one different from the others. It includes everything from light-hearted tales to deep, thought-provoking pieces. This mix keeps the reader interested and offers a chance to experience many different feelings and ideas. Each page brings something new and exciting.

Acknowledgements

My mom and dad were incredibly supportive throughout the process of creating this book, offering their guidance and encouragement every step of the way. I also thank my sister Aisha for her support and belief in my work. Khushnoor's book was the spark that inspired me to start writing, and my brother Saraf played a crucial role in helping me refine my ideas and get this book published. Their combined support and inspiration were essential in bringing this book to life.

1. Meet my Daddy

Meet my daddy
He is the best
He is always glad
That's not so bad
He does many jokes
I laugh all the time
He also sings a rhyme
I love it
I love my daddy Very much
He is such a happy person
You can ever think of
I love my daddy
He spends all day with his phone
But I'm still not alone
He loves a colour which is bright
The colour is white
I love my daddy very much

2. What did corona do to us

Oh my! corona what did you do
You are the worst
Germ to exist !
Go away now !
You are our foe
We suffer because of you
Go away now
You are not a famous germ
You are so lame
Corona warriors
Please help us
Corona please
Go away now
If you don't go
Corona warriors will get you
Thanks corona warriors
Kill corona right now
I hate you corona
I love you corona warriors.

3. Who do I love

Who do I love?
That's a big question
who do I love ?
I have to find that out
I loved someone
I forgot who she is
Someone help me remember
Who I love
She is one of my family member
And my sister
Who do I love
Let me know
She loves me too
Oh !
Now I know who I love
It is my favourite sister
Khushnoor Ali

4. The Story

The little funny story
Written by me
Is about a little bunny
It goes out
In a sunny day
It dances in every way
It goes in a cave
It is the bunny fave
The bunny sees honey
It eats the honey
And becomes funny
What a silly bunny
But wait !
There is something the bunny will hate
But what?
The Bunny will hate
more honey !

5. The Ice-cream fun

Oh my God!
I got a dream
Which is about
Ice cream
It is my treat
The whole town
Is an ice cream town
Let us eat
Ice cream
Tasty yummy treat
I love ice cream
yummy yummy ice cream
I like chocolate ice cream
When it is so sunny and hot
What do we need
We all know what
It is ice cream
Oh boy! It is so hot
I need ice cream
What is your favourite
flavour of ice cream?

6. Fruits and Veggies

Fruits and veggies
Yum yum yum !
Very very tasty
Nam Nam Nam
Be healthy
Be strong
With the help of fruits and veggies
If you are sick
There is a way
To be healthy again fruits and veggies
I am so hungry
I want to eat
Give me some fruits and veggies
Yum yum yummy
I want them right now
Carrots broccoli lettuce beans and cucumber If you are sick you
have to eat veggies
Mango apple orange pear and banana
If you are weak you have to eat fruits
Yummy yum.

7. A Special Flower

A little flower
Very special
Which glows at night
And doesn't glow at daytime
It is very pretty
I look at it triple times
It is so nice
In the night
I see in glow
Just like sunshine
In the daytime
I go to see it again
But it is gone !
Where could it be ?
I ask my mom
She said it is in my house
I see it in a flower pot
I love the special flower

8. The Strange Dream

I got a silly dream
While sleeping
I saw a bunny with
Red little eyes
And stupid dog
Who eats rabbits
It saw the bunny
And ate it up
I was so shocked
When the dog saw me
It licked me with it's
dirty tongue
I ran away from it
I was so scared
Then I saw it running after me
I did not know why
And to my surprise I saw myself
Having a bunny tail
I ran away! I was so scared
Then I woke up with relief
I am glad it was just a dream.

9. Spring

I woke up in the morning
Because spring has come!
Let's have some fun today.
The flowers bloom beautifully
The fruits become ripe.
Spring has come!
It rains in spring.
It is a pleasant season.
Spring has come!
I love spring!
Everyone! spring has come.
Spring is my favourite season.
Everything turns green and fresh.
I love to see the flowers.
I love to eat the ripe fruits.
Spring has come!

10. I am an artist just like my sister

I am an artist just like my sister.
Khushnoor Ali Is an artist like me.
My art is good and sometimes bad.
But I don't care.
I am still an artist.
I can paint, colour and write too.
Just like my sister.
These are my hobbies , that I like to do.
I am an artist!
I can paint, and write anything!
Because I am an artist.
Just like my sister
Khushnoor Ali
But I hate drawing.

11. Colours

Colours are my favourite
I love all the colours.
But my favourite colours are blue, pink, green and white.
I still love all the colours.
The world is so colourful.
The rainbow has colours too.
Red ,orange ,yellow, green ,blue, purple, white, black, pink,
indigo, brown, blonde , golden ,silver are all the colours I love
very much.
These colours are so beautiful
I love all the colours!
In art you can see colours too!
I love colours!

12. My Grandparents

Meet my grandparents
They love me
And I love them too
When I feel blue
They always make me happy.
They are all I need.
Indeed!
I love them so much
They are such happy grandparents.
When I feel bad
They make me glad.
When I have problems in my head
That I can't go to bed
They help me feel better.
I love my grandparents very much.

13. My Family Picnic

Yesterday I had the best day ever,
Which I will never forget!
I had a family picnic , which wasn't very quick!
It was a long day , in a special way
I had to say "best day ever!"
It was a kind of day which was in my mind
We had lovely food
It changed my bad mood.
I get to play in a fun way
I hope I go to a family picnic again!

14. Stars

Stars, stars
Shiny stars, shining bright in the sky
Up so high.
I love the stars.
They are so bright.
They have pretty light.
I look at them every night.
The stars are so shiny and tiny.
I always see them and never stop.
They are so pretty I see them in the city
I love the stars.

15. A Little Teddy

There is a little Ted, who is on the bed .
It is so cute , even if it's mute.
It is so small but, not so tall
I love the teddy
I play with it steady
I really like it , I don't hate it a bit.
It were the suit and a boot too!
She will love you and me so much!
She never say such a thing
She is so kind, she has a lovely mind.
I love the teddy.

16. Meet Me

I'm haiqa.
I am me.
I am a very good dancer
I study in our own English High School
I live in Al Qassmia
I have a father, mother and small sister
I have interest in science.
I am not interested in art.
I like to play the piano.
I love to read books
I have lovely dreams and lovely friends
I have interest in gymnastics
I have a nice singing voice.
I wish to fly in the sky
I also wish to have flexibility
I am funny and pretty
I am me!

17. Ameya episode 1: A sad Day

Once upon a time there was an 8 year old girl named Ameya. She lived happily with her mom.She was kind and a gentle soul. She loved to see things study, once when she was 13 she went out for a walk with her mom. They were on their way until a car hit her mom and she broke her leg. This reminder Ameya about how her dog died due to an accident when she was just a year old. In the hospital she was crying a lot. It was the saddest moment of her life. When her mom woke up she said to her daughter " Ameya dear, my leg will take 3 years to heal. Till that time you have to go to Seattle with your aunt." Ameya agreed and wondered how her life would be in Seattle.

18. Ameya episode 2: Ameya's cousin

When Ameya reached Seattle , she saw her aunt on her way with a girl who was her cousin. When they saw her they told Ameya to come to their house as they heard about her mom broken leg.

Har aunt introduced heart to her daughter whose name was Serah. She was 2 years younger than Ameya. She was 11. They both looked almost identical except for their had purple hair and Serah had yellow hair. They had nothing in common except their love for each other. When Ameya went to her new school, she liked it. It was much better than her old one. There were after school clubs, kind teachers and neat rooms. People were obsessed with her purple hair. This left Serah jealous. When she turned 14 and Serah was 12, Ameya was so shocked as Serah cut her pretty hair badly when she was sleeping.she was angry.

19. Ameya episode 3: A happy smile

Ameya was super upset about her hair.Serah's mom was for the rescue. She gave it a nice Pixie cut and everyone loved it more than before.Serah was angry.Ameya's aunt was so kind her name was Tracey. She was 10 years younger than her mom .Because of her kindness,Ameya felt as if she was in heaven. One day when it was movie time, Serah revealed tracey's secret. She pulled her pretty red hair and it turned out to be a wig. Tracey was so angry that she slapped Serah so hard that one of her front tooth fell. That left Ameya stunned. She put the wig back on her aunt's head and Serah apologized a lot. But she was grounded for a month. When Ameya turned 16 it was time for her to leave Seattle. She would miss her aunt and Serah so much. She asked her mom if she could move there and she gave a big smile when her mom agreed.

20. My Talent

My talent is fun, my talent is interesting
I have a lot of talents
But this is my top talent.
It isn't writing or drawing
It isn't something simple
It is gymnastic dancing!
It took too much practice
But it was worth it
Gymnastics is hard, but fun too!
I want to become a gymnast.
My weakness is art,
I hate drawing
But I do love painting!
My talents are fun!

21. A girl in wonderful space

A girl went to space
To see the bright stars
She is also amazed by the planet Mars!
She also went to space
To pluck a star or two
But she changed her mind
For it would destroy the view.

22. Meet my mom and sister

They are the best
Both of them love me and I love them too.
My sister is sweet and cute.
I call her Bittu .
We might fight but, we love each other
My mom is a kind person
She is kind to everyone
She loves me dearly and wants me to be safe
I have got a loving family
Thank you God!

23. Fantastic school jokes

Want to hear school jokes? Here they are!

What is a snake's favourite subject?

Ans:hissstory

Why did the students eat their homework?

Ans: it was a piece of cake.

In English class, my English teacher asked me "what's new?". I said "an adjective".

Why are fishes so smart?

Ans: they have a school of fish.

24. Ella and Bella

There are two twins
The elder one is Bella
Who loves to race
The younger one is Ella
Who has a pretty face
They have separate rooms
Ella has a pink room
With a pink door
Bella has a blue room
With a blue floor
They both have different hobbies
Ella has a nice hobby
Which is to sing
Bella loves to dance
Which is a nice thing
They both love one another
Like no other

25. Popularity

Popularity is something
Which everyone likes
I know everyone wants
To be popular like others
But are they making the right choice?
Popular people are liked by everyone
They give their fans autographs and they even roast people
However, popularity is temporary
Someone or the other will replace you
Some people might get jealous of you and will find ways to insult
you
Sometimes the best way to get popular is to do the right thing
When you do the right thing
No one will ever forget you
And will always love you

26. A girl with a dress

A girl with no dress
Was in stress
She wanted a lovely dress
She saw a button
Small but high
She tried to be tall
To reach the button
When she pushed the button
She got a dress
But was in stress again
Cause it was in a mess
Oh my !
What did that girl do ?
What was she up to ?
She saw another button to press
But did she be in stress when pressing the button ?
No, she was not in stress
As she got a pretty dress

27. Wind

Wind indeed
Is all we need
When there is a bubble you blow
It will beautifully flow
All thanks to the wind
A boat can sail ,a mail can flow
A kite can fly ,high in the sky
All thanks to the wind
It is the winds pleasure
The wind is our treasure
A fast wind is loud
And it scares the crowd
But not me
I love the wind
Thank you wind for all you do
I love you

28. A Red Ball

I see a red ball
Which is so small
It is so shiny
And kind of tiny
When I have a problem in my head
I can't go to bed
When I see the red ball
I fell much better
I play with it everyday
But it gets lost
No way !
I look for it but can't find it
My kind friend finds it
I scream with joy
I fell so proud
I dance with the crowd
I love my red ball

29. Cool jokes to tell your friends

Here are nice jokes

To tell your friends

What goes up but never come down?

Ans: Your age

What do fruit twins love ?

Ans: Pears

Why did the teacher wear sunglasses to the school?

Ans : Her students were so bright

What did the cow do in the spaceship ?

Ans: It saw the moon

What day do the chicks hate ?

Ans : Fry-day

What do you call a sad strawberry?

Ans: A blue berry

30. The insect and waiter

An insect went to a restaurant
It asked the writer, "do you have any food?"
The waiter said no
The insect came the other day
And asked the waiter
"Do you have any food?"
The waiter said , "if you come to ask me this question again, I
will smack you out with a newspaper. Now get out!"
The next day, the insect wanted to ask for food again but it
said, "do you have a newspaper I could borrow ?"
The waiter said, "no I do not have one "
Then the clever insect asked, "ok, then do you have any food ?"

www.ingramcontent.com/pod-product-compliance
Lightning Source LLC
Chambersburg PA
CBHW020518160726
47991CB00007B/3010